I0190110

Tate's Hell

The Full Story

Other books by Pauly Hart

Supernatural Horror Novels
> By the Gates of the Garden of Eden
> The SRO (In progress)

Short Story Collections
> Sometimes I Write Tiny Stories
> Dreams Both Great and Small
> Adelphoi

Magazine
> Microzine: Volumes 1-5

Novellas and Novelettes
> Superior Respondent
> The Book of Lesser Voices
> Ouesso to Epena
> Mountain to Mountain
> Empire of the Dragon
> The Word of Yahweh unto Enoch

All books are available on
Amazon.com and PaulyHart.com

Tate's Hell
The Full Story

Pauly Hart

All content copyright © 2022 by Pauly Hart and is not available for reproduction, physical or digital without expressed consent from the author. All rights reserved.

Any Characters found inside are fictional and any resemblance to people living is purely coincidental.

Published by Pauly Hart Art

Printed in the USA, where available.

ISBN: 9781955399364

Jacket and Cover Design by Pauly Hart

For information about the author, please visit PaulyHart.com

Library of Congress Catalog Data is available at: Loc.gov

This book is available on Amazon.com

For Christian Niles

Preface

If you head south from Tallahassee on 98 you might end up right in the Gulf of Mexico if you don't follow the road west as it turns down the Florida Panhandle. Stay on 98 as much as you can, and in around 430 miles you can park your car and go to Cafe du Monde for Chicory coffee and Beignets. Parking is free if you're willing to walk a couple of blocks, and it's delicious. The only problem is the line is usually long and you might stand around for 30 minutes or longer.

It's an interesting trip to be sure. It's not often that you can just look out to your left and say: "Hey it's the ocean!" for four hours, unless you live on an island and you're driving in right hand circles. Along the way to New Orleans you'll pass by great beauty and plenty of places to pull over and check out the view. From the haphazard fishing towns, to tourist destinations, from resorts to swamps - it's a fun drive. I should know all of this, because last year we had to bury my wife's grandmother. It was a sad affair, but as most of the family is in Tulsa, Oklahoma and we now live in Savannah, Georgia; several routes were planned but eventually the long beach drive on 98 won the argument.

One of the very first places of interest we encountered started with an odd sign. "Tate's Hell State Forest," it read and left us wondering what in the world was going on. Of course my interest was piqued right from the get-go. Years ago when I lived in Flint, Michigan I had driven an hour out of my way to have my photo taken in front of the sign to Hell, Michigan... Of course I needed to check it out.

The wife got the dog out of the car as we looked at the wide spot on the road where the sign told us we could find Tate and his hell and I said: "Should we go?" And she said: "We really don't have the time." To which I reluctantly agreed. From the road you could see the dense foliage, pushing anyone away who might be insane enough to venture inside. Not all swamps are the same, and this one looked more swampy than other swamps I'd been in. I walked off the road about four feet and that's when the wall of mosquitos decided that my intrusion was to be met with a most vampiric onslaught. Retreating, I said: "Alright! I'm ready!" So, after our dog claimed ownership with his scent on the sign, we loaded back up and drove on westerly to exotic places such as: Apalachicola, Panama City, Destin, Gulf Breeze, Gulf Shores, Biloxi, Gulf Port, and eventually, New Orleans to eat tasty snacks. After all of that, we headed up to Tulsa, getting in really late. We spent time grieving with the family, said our farewells, and in a couple of days, headed back home.

We took the short way home. 40 to Memphis, 22 to Birmingham, 20 to Atlanta, 75 to Macon, and 16 to Savannah. But I never forgot Tate's Hell. I wondered about it for weeks and eventually got so fed up with the lack of information that I did a deep dive on the internet. After finding around 38 places that said the same thing, I had enough. No one had taken the time to chronicle this man's life in total. Oh sure, here and there were mentions that he had a cow, or that his wife was Jewish, or that they traded with the natives. Bit by bit I cobbled together an almost seamless patchwork quilt of who the man was, and how he had lived. I filled in the gaps with general period specific information about swamp life in that era, the mood of the country, and what it would have looked like for Cebe.

And that's what this book is. It's the story as best as anyone can tell it, from all the information that we have. I'm a pretty good story-teller, and an OK researcher, so I've done my best for you, my dearest reader. No, this story has no great moral compass. No, this story has no great heroic outcome. This is one of the most natural, and i'll-fated stories as I'll ever write in my whole career. Raw truth seldom has great story-telling elements in it. Great story-telling relies on devices one rarely sees in real life. The Hero's journey, for instance. Where the "chosen one" after the death of his mentor, goes on and changes his own life to meet the ultimate bad-guy... Yeah. That's reserved for Star Wars, Harry Potter, The Hunger Games, and others like it. Cebe Tate ain't anything like a hero by today's story-telling standards. He's a down-trodden farmer who has the world go wrong at every turn.

It's speculative fiction in its purest form. Hopefully, whatever the actual, full truth is... Isn't far from the story you hold in your hands today. I trust you'll enjoy reading it, just as much as I enjoyed writing it.

-Pauly Hart
November 15th, 2022

Now

It was getting late and Cebe Tate only had three shotgun shells left. He hadn't seen that dratted Mountain Lion for three or four hours. It must have gone farther out into the swamp. Maybe it was up in the trees. But it was somewhere close.

'Blazes', he thought. 'That spit licking cat is probably right behind me.'

He whirled around. The sloshing of his shoes stirred up the swirling mud and grass around his limbs. Scanning the trees he saw nothing out of the ordinary. A small egret sat on the top of a dead Cyprus, looking down at him.

"Yessir. I know it's your swamp. I'm just passing through." He told it.

The egret said nothing, just cocking its weird little head, staring.

He took a moment to adjust his hat. The ear gnats were getting bad again, flying right down into his ears and making him crazy. Gnats were among the deepest hatred of his heart. They had come up from the depths of Hell itself as far as Cebe was concerned. Dad must have made a mistake to make those. There didn't seem to be any point to 'em.

Far away, there a *sploosh* came from one of the deeper parts. He knew it was gators. Had to be - worst case scenario and all. Mayhap it be turtle, but then again, you can't hope for hope's sake 'round this mess. It usually was the worst case. Knowledge like that'll save yer hide, time and time again.

Then

It was late and the wife was making potato cakes again, from the smell of it. The pigs were wrestling some grub that had fallen from the trees and he wanted to check the farrowing pen one last time while there was still light. Walking on the pine straw beds the wife had laid down, he crept up on the hut just to listen. Just the deep grunts of the mama yet. The litter hadn't dropped. It would be soon. Real soon. He had hoped it would have been today but there was no such luck. He decided to peek in anyway. He wanted those fresh piglets to get moved into the new pen he had just bought. He slowly opened the door.

It was the smell first. The mother, nuzzling up some sort of meat was having a go at it. There was blood and remains everywhere all around the farrow hut. She had dropped her litter and devoured them all. The mother looked up at him with disinterest and resumed eating what was left all around.

The savaging was horrible and Cebe was beside himself. He had heard tale of this before but to see it firsthand was revolting.

"You dratted swine demon." He pushed his hat up on his head as tears began to form in his eyes. "Why would you commit such a heinous act of barbarism!? They was yer own chillins!" Placing his hands on the small rail, he leaned hard on it, allowing his shoulders to slump forward and hang his head. Closing his eyes tight, he squinted back the tears and allowed himself to grieve for the lost litter. As he let the grief wash over him, the sounds of the mother still devouring her newly born young were all that was in his mind.

Anger. Deep red hate welled from the innermost parts of his spirit. Like a slow tide or fountain burbling upwards, it came. And it flooded every part of his heart and mind. He clenched tightly to the willow branch of the top rail with all his might. Knotted muscles on his forearms drew tight as he stood there, silent in his rage.

After a minute or so, as the wave subsided, he was able to let go of the rail. His arms ached as he released his fingers and drew his new Bowie from its scabbard, on his hip. He slowly unlatched the gate, came around the busy sow, and slit its throat.

Now

Jasher, the drape-skinned dog licked his hand expectantly. He was a good boy. Samson, his other dog, kept watch out over the swamp. He was a big 'un to be sure, wiry hair dropping over his eyes. Cebe knew he should have shorn Samson last month, but he should do something about it now.

"Come here boy." He said to the big blonde dog. Samson came obediently over. Cebe drew the Bowie from his hip and sawed off several locks from around his eyes. Samson panted happily and very still, knowing that his master cared for him. Samson and Jasher were brothers of the pack, but Samson viewed himself as the caretaker of all. He never questioned Cebe's authority, but when Cebe wasn't around, Samson called the shots. His wife had hated that.

Another *sploshing* down in the deep. It was a gator, no question. Probably finishing its meal. It was getting dark. Here was as good a place as any to sleep. He was tired, no doubt, and was sure that the dogs would keep alert, even through the night, but he wasn't keen on all the mosquitoes around. It was torture, and it wasted a lot of energy, always swatting them away from his face. He figured he could take his handkerchief and maybe drape it over his face to keep them off at night, and maybe keep his hands in his pockets as well. That only left his neck exposed. Even with the collar up, he'd be a feast for them.

And he was hungry. Darned hungry.

He gathered up some of the sphagnum moss from off the raised floor and then set about grabbing down some of the spanish moss from the draperies on the dogwood trees and made himself a bundle. He checked the ground around a big swamp fig for centipede and other burrows. There was nothing… No ants either. He laid out the bundle nice and neat for his posterior and a little extra for a pillow. He wouldn't get his head near the ground, but would lean it up against the fig tree. Bugs in the ears were the bane of his sanity. He didn't need any more of that nonsense.

Jasher inspected his work, as Cebe was finishing and plonked down in the middle of the moss bed. He happily wagged his tail looking at Cebe happily.

"Sorry friend." Cebe said, "That's mine. You sleep there." Pointing to the spot beside it.

Jasher ducked his head and moved silently to the spot Cebe had pointed to, gave a big sigh and lay down, dejected. Cebe loved him. He patted his head and sat down on the bed. Jasher's tail told him he was forgiven and that he loved him as well.

Cebe pulled off his shotgun and bag and laid it beside him.

"Samson!" He called. The dog trotted over.

Cebe pointed to the bag and said: "Guard."

Samson sniffed the bag and gave a low *ruff* that told Cebe he would.

Then

It was too late to slaughter the sow properly. The wife would have complained at him to no end having done it tonight anyway. It was her Sabbath, starting on Friday Sunset, and she demanded they rest. No work would be done, whether in the house or out of it. It was one of the nicer things about her, at least one of the things that bothered him the least. No work meant *no work*. She was adamant about it.

But the sow was dead. He had killed it in anger, even if out of some necessity. He couldn't have this mamma killing every litter she gave birth to. And maybe she wouldn't have. This was her first brood, but he could not afford to take that chance. Bad swine was bad swine.

He was sopped in blood. The fresh cut still poured from the neck of the sow and it was washing over the remains of the litter. There was a small skull in the corner. It was only his steel nerves that held in the contents of his stomach. He would dispatch of the sow the easy way. He would feed it to the younger herd. The sow was from the old herd, on the other side of the clearing, and they might become crazed if they found they were feeding on their former friend.

Maybe not. Darned swine were smart animals, but cold-hearted villains as well. Cebe wanted to be better safe than sorry. That's why he had separated the pins in the first place.

He wiped his hands on the fatty side of the sow, trying to get as much blood off as possible. Coming out of the small furrowing hut, both dogs were standing at the door, expectantly.

"We're alright." He told them. "We're alright." They dogs wagged their tails. Samson trotted off and Jasher sat on his hindquarters. "Just gonna get a rope." He told Jasher.

He knew it was the smell of blood that had brought them over. The cussed sow hadn't made a sound when he dispatched it, maybe it knew it's fate was to come for what it had done. Maybe it was just insane. Who knew?

He walked over to the back of the house, where the tools were, to get a batch of rope. His wife caught his eye, out of the window, and pointed to the sun. He waved his hand at her as if to say: 'I know Sabbath is coming, cool your horse team.' She must have seen his bloody hand but didn't say anything to him.

Finding the rope segment, he brought it back to the furrowing hut and lashed up the sow. It took a lot of work to drag him the 175 feet to the smaller pen but it was worth it. The yearlings and the others were frantic. They knew what was happening. They didn't know how or why, but they could smell the blood.

The whole swamp could smell the blood.

Now

Crack! The swamp rang out. Samson and Jasher were on their feet immediately. Samson, pointing towards the noise gave sharp alert barks. Jasher spun in circles, raising a general alarm. Cebe clamored to his feet as quickly as he could manage, being stiff from his night's sleep. His eyes were bleary, full of gloppy sand and he flung his arms around, looking for shotty. Fingers grabbed it up, brought it to hand, back straightened, stock to shoulder, swinging round, hammer back, aimed at... Nothing.

He looked around slowly, left to right, then back again. Samson was still barking. "Quiet boys." He almost whispered. Samson quit barking but stood pointing in the direction of the noise that had woke him. He watched for a moment and could make out the small ripple in the water where the noise had come from. He waited then it came again. One of the smaller logs in the water suddenly crashed down on top of the water. *Crack,* went the sound. Tarnation. Nothing but the gators in mating. He watched as it raised its tail again and vibrated it violently, then from the other side, he saw the jaws raise and a low *Raaaaaaaaa* come from the creature. He couldn't see the female anywhere but the male sure saw her. Nothing to worry about as long as he didn't come near the female. If he did that, the male would attack. And he wasn't about to be attacked by no gator.

He looked up to where the sky was rising over the trees. Must be around an hour after cock's crow, just now sunrise. He never slept this long at home, he was up with the yard birds usually. It wasn't home, it was the trail, so it was alright. You moved with the day and stopped when you needed. You followed the land. You followed the panther you had to kill. Pulling some pem from his satchel, he broke it off and chewed on it. It was pork pem and it had been awful before he had added the chokeberry to it. They told him that pork pem would never sell, but when he added the berries, he offloaded it pretty darned quick. He was getting pretty good at making it, but didn't have the time any more. Tentoceche had told him to add the berries, just like he had given him the means to make it.

Then

Tentoceche had accepted the two bricks of pine tar Jebediah and Cebe collected with a grin. He pulled off a small bit and rubbed it around on the bottom of his right moccasin, near the toe. It was wearing thin. Tentoceche smiled and placed it back on the brick. Motioning for them to come closer, he laid out his bag on the table next to the bricks. Pulling open a large container of folded leaves, he pulled out two hatchet head slivers, dark brown in color. He motioned for them to eat. When Jebediah and Cebe didn't move, Tentoceche pulled a little from the clutch and put it in his mouth. He chewed for a very long time, smiled, and swallowed with his eyes closed.

Jebediah took the sliver, tore some off and handed it to Cebe. "Eat son." He said.

Cebe took the small piece and sniffed it. It smelled like bison a little. Maybe like the way bison leather would smell. He bit off a little. It tasted a bit like bison meat, but then he'd only had it twice before, so he could be wrong. He smiled and chewed it more. The flavor was like sunrise, the more he chewed it, the more delicious it became. When Cebe eventually swallowed it was the best bison he had ever tasted. Tentoceche smiled and slid the slivers over to them and smiled. Cebe handed the rest of it to his dad who ate it suspiciously. He popped the morsel in his mouth, gave it one good bite, then swallowed the whole thing. Tentoceche laughed. Jebediah was not a patient man.

"So you got jerky." Jebediah said. "Every lickfinger knows haw ta make it."

Tentoceche laughed again and pulled another piece off the sliver. Pulling out his knife, he mashed the wad down flat, around and around until it was almost a large disk, like a sliver of a cut tree. He held it up to the sun. Inside of it, you couldn't see any meat. There were seeds and strands, but no actual meat or fat veins.

"No jerky." Tentoceche said. "Pehmikan. Meat. Fat. May-haw. You call berry."

Jebediah cocked his eye to the tall native. "So?"

"No smoke. No spoil. Bring out. Put together.

Jebediah screwed his face up tight. He didn't speak Muskogee and Tentoceche didn't speak very good English. "How is it jerky if there ain't no smoke?"

Tentoceche smiled and said. "I show you."

Now

Walking for a couple of hours in the swamp was horrible. Walking for days was hell. A Centipede had nabbed him on the trail and had bitten pretty hard on the leg. He had ripped the seam around the bite when he first found it, driven almost mad with pain. That was the dumbest thing he could have done. He managed to worry away some of his shirt collar and use the thread to patch the seam, but it had been exposed long enough that the mosquitos had a go at the blood. Now on top of the centipede bite, there were thirty mosquito bites, making it puff up with an angry red. It stung like Dad's hades, and there was nothing to do for it, except put some ripped cloth on it and itch around the sides like a mad hornet.

He came on an old settlers cabin, with a trail leading to it. He cautioned the dogs to get behind him and approached cautiously.

"Hallo there!" He called out. Dragonflies buzzed happily around the trees. They were the only answer the swamp had for him. "Hallo!" He called again. Still it was only dragonflies who answered.

He creeped up to the house. It was a one room wooden cabin with no front door and the one front window had been busted out. He walked in, shotty at the ready. Samson bounded in after him, trotting around, a low growl under his breath. It had been cleaned out a long time ago. There was a sort of table in the middle and two broken chairs in the corner. There was a bed frame and loose straw and the cupboards were all open. One broken cup was all that remained.

Cebe went to the window and yanked down the curtain and folded it over, and tied it off on the wound. It had gotten on his last nerve, the constant itching as he took each step. He wound it once around his leg, his upper left, and tied it off neat. It took a lot of the pressure off and felt wonderful… As wonderful as a bite like that could feel. He would just have to remember to change out the loose plug of cloth he had shoved in the wound. There was nothing else here and called the dogs to him when he saw the track. On the right, up on the cupboard counter, was a large cougar print in the dust. It had to be Old One Eye's. It just had to be. Cebe put his hand down next to it. It was almost the exact size as his hand. Old Dad was crazy to create such a dratted cuss like that. He would ask Him why He had in the great hereafter. First, Cebe had to kill the cuss, and then ask Dad about it.

There was a splash in the woods and Samson bolted towards the door. Cebe blocked him and shooed Jasper and he away towards the back of the house. He waited, dead silent, looking out at the low branches, swollen roots, and Spanish moss. It was quiet.

Suddenly there was a huge *WHUMP* on the roof. The dogs went insane. Samson howled and yelped bloody murder and Jasper shot outside.

"Jasper! No!" Cebe screamed at him but it was too late. From atop of the house, a dark shape flashed downwards and engulfed the dog.

"Samson! Attack!" Cebe cried and pointed. Samson ran pell mell into the fracas obediently, teeth ready for flesh.

Then

Tentoceche waved his long knife in the air at the retreating white man. His arrow quiver held the three barbed arrows he so proudly made. Tentoceche was a warrior first. Part of the Apalachee people, he had no fear of the white man and their barbed wire. They thought they could own this land with their tree and mud cakes houses. They came in and possessed it like it was theirs to have. No one had the earth.

The white man waved his shotgun back at the Native man. The white man wandered back to his home. Tentoceche worried about him. He was all alone now. His father and wife were gone and there was no one but him here. What if he suffered an accident. Tentoceche resolved to come by twice as often. Maybe the strange white man Cebe would need the company.

Tentoceche remembered Jebediah with fondness. He remembered his son Cebe, so small back then, and teaching them some of the ways of his people. Skills they would need here in the wild swamp of the land. He shook his head. Why did the white man build here anyway? You could not tame this land. It was against the law that nature had made for it. This was the swamp. Not a place for the Tate's cattle or swine. No one in their right mind would try to keep herd animals here.

Tentoceche took one last look at the settlement, put away his knife in its scabbard, and headed away with his small wagon to the next house out here in the swamp.

Now

He held Jasper's body one last time before surrendering him into the small grave he had dug outside the abandoned cabin. He loved that old thing. The cat had done a number on him. Jasper had put up a good fight but by the time Samson had joined them, the cat had basically ruined Jasper's front right leg. The cat had somehow ripped most of the skin off and crushed the bones with his teeth. It was gone and there was no way Cebe could mend it out here in the black wet damp of the green hell. Jasper had also had a long swipe down his right side that would take more than his skill to tend to. There was no other choice. He had used one of his western cartridges and shot down into the ground. It had been clean and quick.

Samson didn't understand and pawed at his life long friend to coax him to move by whining and nuzzling him. Samson tried licking at the deep gashes on Jasper's side and when Jasper didn't move he circled him whining all the more. After Cebe had pulled the trigger he had dug the hole and put him in as quickly as he could, before the flies and other critters got too bad. Blood in the swamp was a rumor all the critters would want to come investigate. Cebe had kicked most of the grave out with his shoes and done the same to bury him. He got as many dead sticks and twigs as he could and piled them on top of the grave as well, hoping the soppy branches would diffuse the smell.

The scar on the tree where he had shot at the cuss still glared white at him, as mockery of his failure. Samson had remained unharmed. Old One Eye had made plans to take Jasper away into the trees for his meal, if it weren't for Samson and Cebe. Samson hadn't got a lick in, and Cebe had wasted on of his good copper shells on the critter. He wished he had more copper or even that parkesine he had heard about, but he had a few paper shells and western cartridges and only 1 more copper. He didn't know if he could even kill the thing with a paper cased shell, maybe it being shot in his face, sure... But that was suicide.

He got all the furniture together inside the cabin and rammed it against the doorway. With a small fire in the old hearth, he would have at least three walls. He would sleep against the back. Three walls were better than none, out there in the green.

He had managed the small fire with bark mostly. Anything to keep the chill off inside the small cabin. Most of the wood was damp and covered in algae and moss. He had tracked the cussed cat this far and weren't gonna stop until he caught him. That dratted thing had killed his cows, his pigs, and everything else he had that was his. He was gonna find it and kill it. It had happened in stages, over time. After he had taken out the four cows, One Eye had taken the pigs one by one, no matter what Cebe had tried, it never worked. He almost had him once... But the cat had learned from that and never repeated the same mistake.

Then

Late at night, he waits in a stand for One Eye. He'd slaughtered one of the sickly sows, one of the older ones in the old pen, and he'd done his best to make sure it was a sloppy job. He'd strung guts up in the trees… A terrifying thing to do, because of all the alligators, but there was no other way about it. Gathering all of the young sows into the farrowing hut, it was crowded to be sure, but it was the only way. Much to his wife's dismay, the older remaining 5 older sows were in the house with the dogs, inside the old closet, with his wife cursing him up and down this way and that about the whole ordeal.

She had almost had enough of every aspect of the ordeal. Her cows, all now dead, had been sold at a loss to the town butcher, for there was so much meat that Cebe hadn't been able to salvage it all in the smokehouse. He'd tried, but the cat had done a number on them night after night. In the course of the last week, the cat had been killing for fun, killing just to kill.

His wife had written to her kin to come collect her, and Cebe would be given a certificate of divorce and the reverse dowry would be due them. But Cebe had no more money. All the money he had was tied up in the now dead livestock. Her family would understand… They had to. There was nothing he could do.

He was quiet while he waited. The low and grumpy grunts coming from the house and the farrowing hut are getting quieter over time and eventually became quiet as the sky turned darker until it was black. He was eaten by the mosquitos and wondered if he would die from their bites. Some folks were saying that's how the Devil's disease was spread… Your skin turning yellow and black pus coming from your eyes... But he didn't believe it. It had to be foul air, or evil vapors... Or both.

A crack in the trees broke him from his reverie; He sensed more than heard the foul beast... A shimmering presence coming from it, making his skin tingle... It was right in front of it. He slowly raised his shotty from where it had been tucked into his ankle, inside his boot. The small tree stand was about twenty feet up in the air. The cat would never expect him to be there.

Finally, the dark shape pauses tenuously at the intestines strung in the trees. It's Old One Eye himself. His dark matted fur mixed in with the half orange marbled fur making him part black panther and part demon. He sniffs the air and yawns big. Cebe can see the teeth from where he is and knows that if those things ever got into him, he'd be done for. He slowly takes aim, raising shotty to his shoulder. It's over. He knows it. It's over now. He moves his hip to the right in the smallest of adjustments and the board creaks with that smallest of movements.

The cat stiffens and Cebe cusses under his breath and fires but the cat is already rushing towards him.

Now

In the morning it is silent, there is no cat, there are no other animals moving. It's just the bugs, Samson and himself. He struggles to get up. His leg aches something fierce and his stomach grumbles for almost a full minute. He checks his little bag and there's his handkerchief and some shells. When did he eat the rest of his food? Oh that's right, he had a dream he ate it all. It must not have been a dream. Samson licks his chops.

"What?" Cebe asks. Samson responds by bounding over and licking his face. Crumbs fall to the floor and he grabs those up as well. Cebe had eaten every bite in his sleep. That sounded like him alright.

"Well boy, let's find some frogs or something." He says and tries to stand but the pain in his leg about knocks him on his back. He yelps out in pain and checks his bandage. Removing it hurts like tarnation but he gets it off and it's black and red and streaked. *Hells bells*, he wonders, *Didn't I change this yesterday? How long have I been out here?* He honestly doesn't know. It must be a little while more than what he thought.

"All the food is gone." He told Samson. The dog wags his tail, because the master loves him and will figure out where to get food.

"I gotta change this out." He examined the wound. It was pretty bad and only getting worse. There was no water anywhere that was fit to clean it, and he had no pot to boil any. He would just have to find the creature and get back home.

Where was home?

He got up and took all the broken furniture away from the door. There were cougar prints everywhere.

While he slept, he was being sussed.

Old One Eye knew him now.

There had to be an end to this madness.

He threw the remaining furniture away and poked his head out, looking around, then up at the trees, then above his head at the roof.

It's nowhere to be seen.

Then

He was young back then. Not even a man. The preacher had come from town and helped with the ceremony. One of the distant neighbors had helped his father dig the hole, but he insisted that he and his boy would close her up. His father had spent a whole $12 on the casket, but his mother had made him promise to buy one. She didn't want to wind up in the dirt in her pretty dress.

It wasn't a pretty dress. But it was the only one she had.

And they buried her in it.

His father took off her wedding ring and her locket necklace before they nailed her in.

Later he gave the ring and the locket to the preacher and promised him a hog in a month.

Even the funeral had to be borrowed to be paid for. Such was the poverty of the Tate's.

He remembered the dress and the way her face sagged.

Such a pretty cornflower blue and such a husk within it.

His father cried at the funeral but never cried again.

That was the only time he ever cried that Cebe saw.

During the day, they worked in silence, Cebe would clean the stalls and Jed would milk the cows, and collect the eggs. When there was too much milk, Cebe churned it... Otherwise this was their meals. Once a week a girl from the market would come over and Jed would load up what eggs he had fresh and all the milk they had and butter as well. Often the eggs would be found burrowed in nests not near the coop and Cebe would catch a licking for missing them. His job was to not let them lay outside the coop otherwise they would be fertilized and be well into hatching. The few that Jed wanted to keep, he'd give to his best hen and the others he'd feed to the goats.

The pigs were a later addition to the little farm. It started out as two, a sow and a boar, and soon enough there were too many of them. They'd eat anything, and that was dangerous and often they'd find chickens disappeared or most of the eggs devoured. This was how they lost their one guinea, their thirty chickens, and a kid, new from the birthing nanny. His dad had cussed the swine for killing the goat, but then again, they should have built them a new pen. Except the goats never stayed in their pen anyway. Who was to blame?

Cebe blamed the inquisitive kid.

Late in the night, when he was laying in bed and smelled the whisky, his father cried out to Dad, "Why oh why oh why God? Why oh why?"

Now

Cebe tracks the cat. His paws are easy to find, now that he's memorized what they look like. He's cleaned the shotty with that old nasty rag he uses. His leg hurts something fierce and Samson is hungry. The last part is sort of taking care of itself. He's gotten a couple of frogs for some quick sustenance, *He's such a good boy,* thinks Cebe. *Hasn't complained about Jasper since I ended him.*

The path he was following was almost too easy. Old One Eye had padded along a deer trail as plain as could be. There was no mistake about it. Maybe this part of the swamp didn't have a road except this one. But he couldn't believe his luck anyhow. Any minute and I'll pop him. Then my life will get back to normal.

This was the perfect time for an angry alligator to show it's horrible head and try to snatch at him. He hadn't been paying attention to right here, right now, which almost did him in. *Rrrrrr!* It growled as it made a lung for him. He wasn't smarter than the gators in their own land, but he was fueled by survival instinct. Hopping up like a hare he scrambled partway up a tree near him. Samson scampered away, nearly frightened to pieces.

Cebe had shotty loaded and ready and *Kapooom* put the alligator down.

If only that dratted cuss were so easy to kill, dagnabit.

Then

He had alarmed the cat to his whereabouts and it had come for him, up in that tree, what seemed like so long ago. It had leapt up the tree quick as lightning and Cebe had fired, missing it, but scaring the literal feces out of it. Cebe had figured the cat had never been so close to gunfire. Obviously he had heard it in the distance, just being on the fringes of the town and all, but probably reckoned it for thunder. Being so close to it, he froze and soiled himself.

Freezing in midair does a couple of things. If you're mid-climb, then you'll lose your balance. And that's what happened to One Eye. He seized up and fell down like he was dead. It took Cebe a couple of heartbeats to realize that he hadn't shot him and to begin to reload the single shot break long rifle. But by the time he'd reloaded, the cat had shaken himself awake and ran off into the bog.

When he came to his senses from the near death experience, Cebe was hugging the tree, shaking and sweating. The dogs were going ballistic and the wife was cursing at all the racket. Of course the hogs inside the house were also slamming up against the walls, terrified. She came out of the house screaming in Yiddish, throwing pots and pans into the yard, a little insane.

That had been the last straw for her. She had written her letter. He was made to sleep in the kitchen the rest of the month until her brother's family came and got her.

Now

He came upon the sleeping cat midafternoon the next day. He had slept on the trail just a little, full of fury and vengeance. There was only hate within his heart. Hate for the dratted thing that had cost him the fullness of life. It had cost him his father. It had cost him his wife. It had cost him his farm. He could not believe his luck. Here was that damned thing right in front of him. Or... Wait.

It wasn't Old One Eye. This was smaller... Wait.

There were two of them. No. There were three of them. Drat. They were cublings. Almost mature enough to be out there on their own.

It all came together in Cebe's' mind. That's why Old One Eye always killed so much recently. She was feeding her cubs. She was only doing what she had been told to do by Dad. Following her nature.

Drat. Cebe thought. *And here I go wanting to kill her.*

And then another voice inside him said: *Damn straight I want to kill that sum-bitch.*

The first voice responded, *She's a mother. She was only doing what Dad told her to do.*

To which the voice replied, *Just like the Methodist gal lied to me.*

Cebe thought, *Well she was straight out lying ta me.*

Oh and what that cat is doing is any better? The voice asked.

Nah, it's worse, but at least it's honest. Cebe said.

"Now go away." He said out loud.

All the cats looked at him.

"Feces." Cebe said, took aim and shot the one closest to him.

He ran back down the trail, Samson leading the way. Smart dog.

He reloaded as he ran, chambering whatever his hand grabbed.

Paper round. He turned and fired. Another hit, the second cat was down and the third quit pursuit.

He ran a little more ways then stopped, reloaded and turned back in pursuit.

"Samson!" He called.

The dog, going farther back the way they had come, turned heel and doubled back at high speed.

Just then, Old One Eye hit Samson from the side and they both tumbled into the water, off the trail.

Cebe redoubled and ran towards them, reloading as he ran. He felt it. A copper shell. Probably his last one. Just as he reached them, he was shoved onto the trail by a massive force from behind.

The last cub sank it's claws into his back as he fell to the ground.

Then

He had pleaded with her then. "Don't go, my love." He had told her, as she stood there, arms crossed, not looking at him. "When the damned cat attacked the first time and I lost my father, you were the only salvation in my heart." She had said nothing, looking at her brother instead.

They had loaded her and her few belongings into the cart and that was the end to it all. He barely saw them driving away,his now former nephew in the back of the cart, waving at him. His wife, sitting on the front bench, facing away from him and towards her life outside of the swamp. There had been a week of grieving for him, but the cows' lowing told him that just because he was hungry was no reason to treat the animals inhumanely. They still needed their food and their care. Two of the cows quit producing. That was fine. He sold them to the market at a fair sum and had a little pocket money for some much needed repairs around the house.

He threw himself into work. He made his father and mother new matching headstones. He ventured into town after a bath and ate supper one or two nights a month at the saloon. There were no available women there, but he kept looking. Everyone of the women anyway knew of his ill fortune anyway and even if he were the most dapper man there, none would have anything to do with him.

So he threw himself into church instead. It was a Methodist place and the women were either too young or old maids. The one woman who was available had told him that she was spoken for by a man from New York City. He knew that was a blatant lie, because of the way the women looked at her, slightly aghast, and then at him and then back at her, with understanding. He did not go back to the church. No one wanted to marry a poor swamp farmer who had ran off the only Jew this town had ever known. No one wanted Cebe Tate. Even the men in the saloon.

THe old Indian came and went, he said he worried about him, but he never stayed to talk and never shared Cebe's table. He was no real friend. He was a trader, only interested in coin.

He had no friends anywhere.

He had but one reliable thing in his life, and that was the cat who wanted to kill him.

Cebe would wake up in the night, jump into his shoes and out the door faster than the wind, only to see the cat leaping over the fence with another sow, time and time again.

He'd tried the tree stand four more times but it was so expensive to slaughter, and besides, the cat already knew that trick.

He would have to hunt the cat to his death. He would hunt it and kill it, and put an end to the devilry once and for all.

Now

The pain rushed through Cebe's head like a waterfall of fire. The cub was still young enough not to understand how to bite the neck to finish him off immediately, but it would figure it out pretty quickly given time. Cebe didn't have that time. Cebe twisted himself to try to get the hurtful end of his shotgun towards the cub. Any part would do, if he could just get the shot in. As he twisted to the right, the left claws ripped his shoulder on down to the blade and he screamed in agony. This alarmed the cub, as it wasn't used to its prey screaming at him and it retracted its claws trying to understand this new situation.

Cebe worked the shotgun back around towards its head and pulled the trigger.

The shower of the bits from the brain pan colored the swamp a fine pink mist.

One Eye shrieked and Samson yelped in unison. Cebe wasn't turned their way so didn't know if they were reacting to him or to each other. He rolled and pushed up onto his stomach and reached for his satchel which held all his ammo. It wasn't there. He couldn't see it anywhere.

Directly in front of him was One Eye and Samson. One Eye had its front right paw up, poised to bat at Samson, who was low, head reared, aiming for the throat of the cat.

He looked to the right for his bag, nothing.

Looked to the left, nothing.

One Eye screamed. She batted at Samson as he went for the kill shot, lunging with all his might at the cat's throat. They were both in four or five inches of water and he must have slipped on his push off because he didn't make it and she caught him and sent him flying off away from him. She turned and pounced on him before he could recover.

Cebe found the bag and almost dove for it. It was behind him, the strap under the cub he had just dispatched. The whole mess was adjacent to a bald cyprus tree with a massive root system. Reloading as quick as he was able, he thought to turn towards where he thought the cat was as he looked up and down from his reloading. The contents were all spilled out and the only ones in the bag were the paper rounds with the scatter shot in them. He searched the bag for a copper. Wasn't there one left? Had he used them all? What about the cartridge shots?

Samson made a sound Cebe had never heard before. It was a yelp of pain so profound Cebe knew it had been his last. He looked up in time to catch the One Eye turning from Samson and looking directly at him. Without looking down, he grabbed a shell and shoved it into the gun.

The shell broke open and showered down on the ground and into the gun. A soggy paper shell.

Drat.

He looked down at the bag. There was only paper shells there.

Looking up, the cat was gone.

Looking left, looking right. No cat.

The cat was nowhere.

He loaded the driest paper shell he had. There was nothing else to it. He had to.

He would only have one shot.

Then

It is much later than Tentoceche realizes when he comes upon the Tate cabin. Mystified as to strange scene before him, he ventures into the cabin calling greetings as he does. He knows he will find no one there, but still inside he goes. The place is a mess, remnants of a man gone partially mad with hatred. He sees the letter on the table in the kitchen and knows he must read it. It will be from Cebe Tate. It will hold the answer to the mystery of what he is seeing.

Dearest Mother and Father,

Though you are not here with me, I do not know who else to address this letter to, as there is no one left for me to tell. As you know, viewing my poor life from the kingdom of Dad's abode, I have not fared well in these last years. Abigail has left me, returning to her people, and the farm is a ruin, brought upon by the evil vex Dad has cursed me with.

The cougar, Old One Eye, as Father named her, has taken all I have save three sows and one hog I have released into the swamp, so that they may begin their life over, away from the hands of man. I was not able to keep them. Nor was I able to keep the cows nor any of the other stock Father had worked so hard to maintain.

I am at a loss as to what to do. So now I seek my revenge upon the beast I have been cursed with, and will hunt it until it lays dead at my feet.

This is all I have become. I am now a wreck and ruin of the son your raised.

May the peace of Dad keep you away from my damnable actions of hate.

Your son,
Cebe Tate.

Tentoceche folds the letter up and replaces it on the table and leaves the way he came. He thinks better of it and returns with a pouch of Pehmikan and leaves it on the table.

Maybe Cebe will return.

He will need help.

Now

He sees a dark shape from the corner of his eye. It's a blur and it's on him before he knows it. Raising the shotgun, it shoves him into the tree, Cebe closes his eyes reflexively but does not die instantly. He opens them in time to see it's bleeding. Samson got a good bite on the front forepaw of One Eye. He's been slammed into the deep roots of the bald Cyprus and the shotgun is parallel to the ground, with both One Eye's paws on it. It's crossways so it's stuck on the extension of the roots, giving Cebe around a foot in front of him.

The pressure of the big demon cat is keeping shotty in place and the cat's left paw is on Cebe's right hand, claws in deep. They're both stuck there. There's no way for Cebe to move shotty to aim it at the cat without immediately being crushed.

"Come on you summbitch!" Cebe screams at the enormous face of One Eye.

One Eye knows something is wrong but doesn't understand the crossbeam keeping him from Cebe. He reaches out with his head, going for Cebe's throat and pushes down, causing the shotgun to slide down along the roots, shoving Cebe in a crouch. The angry mother of the three cubs is going to exact a horrible recrimination upon Cebe in seconds.

But the seconds change for Cebe. Time seems to slow down. In microseconds, all of his body tells him their story. His back, fresh with claw marks from the third cub are screaming at him, being rubbed raw against the tree. His arms hurt from the constant mosquito welts. His neck, his face. His leg hurts from the centipede wound that he never fully tended. His right side has a branch poking up in it now, a new pain.

And here, of all places, memories flood his mind. He recalls his father teaching him how to skin a squirrel. He's in pain. His father holds the knife and with one quick flip, opens up the squirrel to splay the intestines. The branch pokes him even deeper.

That's no branch.

That's his bowie knife.

He pulls it from the scabbard and plunges it with all his might.

End

Long shadows cast an inky spill onto the otherwise quiet Sunday morning in Rio Carabella. The Salem Baptist church bells are ringing for folk to come in to worship. Sunday school has just gotten out so the children are playing in front of the church in and around the hitch posts down the lane. The horses are whinnying but it's not the children. No. It's something else.

The horses smelled him first. Around the corner by the trough, a shambling thing dressed like a man stumbles into the street, leaning on an old ruined shotgun. He walks up to the church, and there, by the front steps, collapses into a heap.

Women scream, little children cry and cling to their mothers.

"It's the devil!" Someone coming out of the church says.

"It's a man!" Someone screams.

"Quick! Get the doctor!" Another one yells.

Clatters and running. Some folk running into the church, and some running out of the church. Deacons and pastors and choir members alike all crowd around. The doctor, on his way to the church already, rushes in and crouches down next to the man.

He is shaking and blood torn and the doctor pulls out his flask and gives the man a sip of whiskey.

"Let's get him into the church," the doctor says, looking at those around him.

They try to raise him to his feet but a sheet of skin slakes off onto the ground, bringing with it a large splashing of blood and gore. It pours out black blood.

They cringe and recoil at the man, but a few lift him and manage to carry him over to the front of the church where there is clapboard, so he is no longer lying in the dust.

"Mister! Mister!" The doctor slaps his face to get his attention. "Who are you? Where did you come from?"

The shredded man manages to focus his eyes on the doctor. He grabs the doctor with a hand and pulls him close to his mouth.

"My name is Cebe Tate and I've just been through Hell."

www.ingramcontent.com/pod-product-compliance
Lightning Source LLC
Chambersburg PA
CBHW021120020426
42331CB00004B/557